STALKED BEYOND *Her* HORIZONS

Stacey Koog

Contents

Chapter 1

In the Beginning

It was the summer of 1996, and Brigitte had just moved back to her native state of Texas to be close to her family after living alone in Virginia. Although she was excited to be around her family—her mother especially—she knew she wouldn't stay in Texas for too long. She began searching for an entirely different state, one that promised great housing, good food, beautiful scenery, and plenty of beaches. Brigitte decided to move to Tampa.

Her mom's boyfriend, a long-distance truck driver, offered to move Brigitte down to Florida, a state he knew well. Together they set out on the road, headed toward what is clearly known today as the Sunshine State. She was eager to get down to Florida and begin her new life. Through her own research, she found a local apartment complex on the north side of town.

The complex offered many amenities Brigitte wanted, including a beautiful man-made lake located at its center. As a single woman, she decided it would be best—and safer—to choose a second-floor unit. Luckily, the complex had a one-bedroom apartment with a view of the lake located on the second floor, and Brigitte snatched it right up.

After settling into her new place, she thought it would be a good idea to become familiar with her surroundings and the neighborhood she had chosen. On a hot summer day, Brigitte drove down the street to a small strip that included a local 7-Eleven convenience store, a dry cleaner, a nail shop, and a pet grooming salon. Brigitte went into the 7-Eleven to purchase a bottle of water and a pack of peanut M&M's. After paying for her items, she decided to go to the dry cleaner next door, knowing she would be bringing in quite a bit of clothing since she worked in corporate offices as an administrative assistant at the time.

When Brigitte walked in, she was greeted by the owner of the cleaner, Diane. Brigitte introduced herself, sharing a little about her background and mentioning that she was new to the Tampa area. Diane was delighted to meet her and assured her that not only did Tampa have much to offer, but the entire state was a gem with plenty to do. Brigitte dropped off a few items and told Diane she would return in a few days to pick them up.

Afterward, Brigitte got into her car and drove off. Much to her surprise, she was being watched from afar by a local man clearly captivated by her natural beauty. He was Caucasian, and Brigitte was Black. He had first noticed her when she was at the 7-Eleven, standing two people behind her in line. He noticed Brigitte's thick thighs as she was wearing shorts and her full breasts in a sleeveless yellow top. Her long hair—extensions she wore that summer—combined with her golden complexion and natural beauty made her all the more striking. Although he was White, he was no stranger to dating Black women. He paid for his items and went to sit in his car and watched Brigitte go into the dry cleaner.

Waiting patiently, he watched as Brigitte drove off. Then he went inside the dry cleaner to ask the owner, Diane, about the young lady who had just left. Diane hesitated, unsure who this man was or whom he meant, until he began to describe Brigitte. Finally, Diane replied, "Brigitte—she's new in town."

The guy asked if Brigitte was married or single. Diane answered, "Single, I think."

He then said, "If I leave my business card with you, can you give it to Brigitte when you see her again?"

Diane said, "Yes, I will pass it on."

He took out one of his business cards and wrote a short note on the back that said, "If you have time for a friend give, me a call. David." He also included his home number as well.

After David left, Diane pulled out the invoice ticket she had given Brigitte earlier that morning and called her. "You have an admirer," she said. "This guy told me he was watching you from outside the whole time you were here and waited until you left so he could give me his number to pass on to you."

Thus the stalking began. Outraged by this guy's behavior, Brigitte drove back to the cleaner, where Diane confirmed that David had indeed left his business card, asking Brigitte to phone him.

Brigitte sat for a while at the cleaner, asking Diane what her first impression of David had been. Diane replied that he seemed fine—dressed in a shirt and tie, suggesting he worked in an office of some sort. She added that she hadn't detected anything strange or unsettling about him.

Afterward, Brigitte drove back to her place. At first, she wasn't sure if she should call David, but she couldn't shake the thought that his tactics had been unruly toward her. Finally, she dialed his number. The phone rang twice, and on the third ring, a calm male voice answered, "Hello."

"May I speak to David?" Brigitte asked.

"This is he," he replied.

Brigitte confronted him right away by saying, "Do you make it a habit of going around giving your card to strange women you know nothing about?"

David replied and said, "If they're as pretty as you."

She went on to tell David that she didn't appreciate his methods. "Instead of asking Diane to give me your card, if you saw me first, you should have been the one to hand it to me."

David apologized, saying he hadn't meant to offend her but simply wanted the opportunity to meet her or talk to her. Brigitte ended the conversation by stating that she was not interested in meeting anyone just yet, as she had only recently moved to the area and was still new in town.

Over the next several weeks, however, David called Brigitte continuously. He was persistent when it came to Brigitte. In each conversation, he would always ask her to go out with him, but Brigitte would decline his offers.

On one occasion, David invited Brigitte to his office on a Friday because his phone carrier, Sprint, offered free long-distance calling that day. He suggested she could call her family and friends back in Texas for free, but she declined. On another occasion, he invited her to do her laundry at his house, knowing she didn't like using the complex laundromat. Again, Brigitte turned him down. She had never met a guy so determined to win her over—or at least persuade her to go out with him.

After several attempts to turn David away, Brigitte went to see Diane, the owner of the cleaner. By this time, the two women had become friends. Brigitte asked Diane what she should do. "David keeps asking me out, and I've told him no." Brigitte added that she didn't want to get serious with anyone just yet, as she wanted the opportunity to meet and date other guys.

Diane then made a mere suggestion to Brigitte. She said, "Hey, just go and have one cup of coffee with this guy. If you get a bad feeling about him, or you don't get a good vibe, then you can end it right there. And all he would have spent on you was $1.25 for a cup of coffee. No big deal."

Taking Diane's advice, Brigitte called David. "I will go out with you," she said, "but only for a cup of coffee and nothing more." Excited that she had agreed, David asked if he could come to her apartment to pick her up. Brigitte said that would be fine.

It was a beautiful Sunday evening when David came to pick up Brigitte. He asked if she had ever been to the port in Tampa. "No, I haven't," she replied. "I want to take you there," he said, "so you can see it while we drink our coffee."

They stopped at a local Dunkin' Donuts. David ordered a large coffee with four creams and no sugar, while Brigitte ordered a medium coffee with four creams and six sugars. As David drove toward the port, he began asking Brigitte about herself. She told him she was born and raised in Texas, her mother and family still lived there, and that her brother Jason was in Virginia, the state she had just moved back from. She added that she had been married once before, briefly, but had no children from that marriage.

David told Brigitte that he grew up in the St. Petersburg area with family members. He also admitted that he was currently dating three other Black women while pursuing Brigitte. Brigitte responded firmly, telling him she was not interested in sharing. "If you want to be with me, you'll have to say goodbye to all those other ladies," she said.

David began to chuckle and laugh. He said to her, "That's not a problem."

It was about a thirty-five-minute drive to the port, and when Brigitte got out of the car, David guided her to a particular spot where they could sit and have their coffee. It was a gorgeous evening—the sun was beginning to set, seagulls circled above the water, swooping down to catch peanuts tossed by people passing by. A mild breeze drifted through the port, and the current kept the waves low and steady. Several couples and families were out enjoying themselves, and Brigitte felt a little more relaxed and calm.

As the evening went on, David shared his line of work. He was involved in money markets, and he told Brigitte that he enjoyed making people money while profiting from those sales himself. As the evening drew to a close, David asked Brigitte, "Could we go to another place I'd like to show you?"

She replied, "No, I'm good with seeing the port." But David insisted that if she like the port, she would love this other place, which was within walking distance. So she agreed, and they both set off, heading north of the port.

While walking, the conversation stayed pleasant. David, of course, kept it clean and classy when it came to talking to Brigitte, wanting to impress her. As they continued to walk, they suddenly approached a beautiful shop that seemed almost enchanted, tucked into the woods like something out of a novel. It was a small café nestled among the trees, called Jeff Desserts.

The moment Brigitte walked in, she saw wall-to-wall glass cases filled with every type of dessert imaginable. Whatever your taste buds craved, Jeff's had it. Brigitte was completely overwhelmed and deeply impressed with David for choosing such a magnificent place.

She turned to him and said, "Okay, this was a very good idea," and smiled at him.

She had not been accustomed to seeing so many desserts or nearly that many. As a native of Texas, she was used to homemade sweet potato pie, lemon pound cake, and German chocolate cake—traditional desserts of her home state. But this café was a haven for anyone with a sweet tooth.

David leaned over to Brigitte and asked, "Do you know what Florida's famous dessert is?"

She replied, "No, I don't."

He told her, "Key lime pie—it's the state's top dessert." They both laughed and ordered their desserts.

Once they finished, David drove Brigitte back home. It was well after nine o'clock by the time she arrived. David walked her up the stairs to her front door, told her he had a great time, and said good night.

The following morning, David called Brigitte. He reminded her of what a good time he had and said he was looking forward to seeing her again. Shortly afterward, David and Brigitte were officially a couple, happily dating.

Over the next several weeks, David exposed Brigitte to all the excitement Florida had to offer. They took day trips to St. Augustine and drove down to Daytona Beach. David, being a spontaneous type of guy, was never boring. He lived life to the fullest and wanted Brigitte right there by his side.

David enjoyed fishing, so he took Brigitte on a boat expedition. But Brigitte wasn't used to being on the open water, and she quickly became seasick. The fact that she couldn't swim didn't make things easier. The waves struck the boat too hard, and Brigitte grew even sicker. Cornered, David asked the captain to take them back to shore, as she was not feeling well at all.

David often lavished her with fancy dinners after work or on weekends. He went out of his way to make Brigitte feel as comfortable with him as possible. As their relationship grew, their intimacy was on point. Because Brigitte was not married, she always protected herself when it came to sex and made sure David wore protection. Getting pregnant before marriage was not the way she had been raised.

Brigitte came from a very traditional family. Her parents had been married for twenty-five years when her father passed away in 1990, during her senior year of high school. She carried that tradition with her, wanting the same kind of lasting marriage her parents had shared.

Chapter 2
The Dating

As each week passed, Brigitte and David found themselves growing closer. Although Brigitte had her own apartment and David his own condo, he felt it was time they stopped sleeping apart. Brigitte often spent the night on weekends and sometimes during the week, but David wasn't completely satisfied with that arrangement. He wanted Brigitte in his home, in his bed, every night.

So one evening, while Brigitte was at David's, she cooked them dinner, and afterward they planned to watch a movie they had rented from Blockbuster. David jokingly said, "If it's too late to drive home, why don't you stay the night?

She said, "Okay, I will."

Then David went for the kill. "Why don't you spend the night every night?"

Brigitte then looked at David and said, "What are you trying to tell me, David?"

He replied, "I want you to move in with me."

Shocked at first—since David had never mentioned this before—Brigitte said, "We're not married, and two people shouldn't be living together unless they're married."

David said, "All right, that's something I can work on, if you'll let me."

Brigitte paused and told him that although she had enjoyed the time they had spent together, moving in was a huge step, and they had only been going out for three months. David went on to explain his feelings, reassuring her that she was the only woman he wanted to be with and that he cared for her deeply.

Brigitte told David she would need some time to think about it, as she had just moved into her own apartment and signed a six-month lease. David replied by saying, "I understand."

But as the weeks passed by, David grew more and more agitated, repeatedly telling Brigitte that he was ready to take the next step in their relationship and wanted to prove it to her.

Brigitte believed David was serious about her, yet she hadn't been raised to shack up with a man she wasn't married to. She fought against her own feelings and told David she would when the time felt right.

Up until this point, the two lovebirds were definitely in tune with each other. One Saturday, David suggested that he and Brigitte drive down to an area called Small Town, just outside Orlando. Brigitte loved Small Town; they had stopped there once before on their way to SeaWorld. It was a small community with several small shops owned by the locals. You could buy just about anything—from T-shirts to jewelry to surfboards—you name it, they offered it. There were also some nice restaurants where you could grab a quick bite, walk around, and take in the sights.

David and Brigitte arrived in Small Town around four-thirty that afternoon, as it was well over an hour's drive from Tampa. As soon as they got out, Brigitte headed straight for the shops. She loved jewelry and was especially interested in sterling silver at that time. She bought a couple of bracelets and a ring, while David went to check out some of the surfboards. He often said he wanted to take Brigitte surfing with him. He wasn't a professional surfer, but he was eager to give it a try or two.

Brigitte couldn't swim and told David that she had nearly drowned as a child. "You will never get me in open water like that," she said. "I can't swim."

David laughed and said, "I'll have to teach you."

Brigitte shook her head and said, "Forget about it. Not going to happen."

As the evening progressed, the two grabbed some dinner and waited until nightfall so they could ride the Ferris wheel. Small Town had one of the best carnivals in the community. Cotton candy and popcorn were Brigitte's favorites whenever she went to the carnivals, and she loved the atmosphere Small Town offered.

It was very late when David and Brigitte left and headed back to Tampa. Brigitte suggested they stay the night at her place since it was closer than David's home, and they agreed. It was well after three in the morning when they reached Tampa. Brigitte told David she was going to take a quick shower, brush her teeth—but not floss—and get into bed before sunrise.

After she settled in, about ten minutes later, David became frisky with Brigitte. She told him, "It's late. I'm not in the mood. I'm tired from today's events. Maybe another time."

But David was persistent when it came to being intimate with Brigitte. He nibbled on her ear, kissed her neck, and said, "Please, baby, I just want to feel you and be with you."

Brigitte repeated, "Go to sleep."

Yet David wasn't having it—he wanted sex and wasn't going to give up until she gave in. Finally, after fifteen minutes of constant kisses and caresses, she gave in.

Up until this point, Brigitte had always practiced safe sex with David. But on this particular night—or morning—in the heat of passion, they didn't use a condom.

Over the next two weeks, Brigitte grew more excited as she prepared to participate in her best friend Nikki's wedding back home. Nikki and Brigitte had been friends since high school and college, and Brigitte was delighted to be part of Nikki's wedding and share in such an amazing experience with her.

David and Brigitte set off to drive down to Texas two days before the wedding. Living out of state, Brigitte didn't get a chance to attend the rehearsal with everyone else, but she managed to squeeze in one day of practice before the big day.

It was a beautiful ceremony, and Brigitte was so happy to see her best friend tie the knot. Afterward, she introduced David to everyone, and together they danced the night away. She only had a brief moment to see her family and introduce David to her mother before they had to hit the road back to Florida, as both were due at work.

While driving back, David asked Brigitte did she enjoy herself at home. She answered yes. David then asked if she had enjoyed the wedding, and Brigitte said, "Yes, David, I did."

When they got back to Tampa the following weekend, David came home with a bouquet of flowers for Brigitte. He told her he was ready to make a commitment. He took out a small box and inside was a ring. He got down on one knee and proposed to Brigitte. She happily accepted. Now it was official—David and Brigitte were engaged.

In the days that followed, Brigitte suddenly began feeling sick at work. One day she felt lightheaded; another day she was nauseous.

At first she didn't think anything of it, but as the days passed, Brigitte grew increasingly sick and began having nosebleeds. One day, she had to leave work and go home to change because blood had gotten on the dress she wore that day to work. That evening, David told Brigitte he was going to pick her up and take her to a nice restaurant near Largo after work. Brigitte agreed and met David downstairs from her job.

When they arrived at the restaurant, the hostess greeted them and seated them by the water, as David loved being near it. The waiter came to take their drink order, and since Brigitte wasn't feeling well, she ordered a 7-Up to calm her stomach a bit. After Brigitte took only two sips, she began to feel horrible—her stomach became nauseous again, she felt dizzy and lightheaded. She told David she didn't feel good at all. David asked, "Should we leave and go home?" Brigitte said yes. By this time, Brigitte had moved in with David and was living with him. On the way home, she asked him to stop at a local Eckerd, now known as CVS.

Brigitte never thought she might be pregnant, as she and David had always used protection. She was careful and responsible, making sure they were being careful, but she needed to be able to rule out every possibility before she seeing a doctor.

David stopped at the Eckerd not far from his home, and Brigitte went inside and bought four pregnancy tests. On the way back, David asked Brigitte how long she had been feeling sick. She said about two weeks, but the symptoms kept getting worse. She just wanted to make sure she wasn't pregnant.

When they got home, Brigitte read the instructions on the tests and decided she would take them the following morning. Morning came, and Brigitte got up and went into the kitchen to start the coffee. She pressed the button and went into the bathroom to perform the pregnancy test, never thinking the possibility she could be pregnant. She laid all four tests on the bathroom counter, dropped a sample of urine on each stick, and left the bathroom. She went into the bedroom to make the bed, folding the blankets and putting them gently back into the closet.

After the bed was made, Brigitte returned to the bathroom to check the results. Lo and behold, all four tests showed positive. At first, she stood there in disbelief, not understanding how this could have happen. Recapping all the times she and David had been intimate, and knowing she had worn protection, Brigitte thought there was no way this could be. She sat on the toilet, trying to think long and hard, and then it came to her: that late night—or early morning—when she and David returned from Small Town. That night David had been persistent about having sex. Brigitte, tired from all the activities, just wanted to sleep, but David wanted her, so she gave in and didn't use a condom that night.

After realizing how she had become pregnant, she called David into the bathroom. David asked if she was all right. She pointed to all four tests.

David said, "What does this mean?"

She said quietly, "I'm pregnant."

David was ecstatic and overwhelmed with hearing this. He began to sing this little chant: "We're happy, we're having a baby. OMG, I'm gonna be a father!"

Brigitte sat quietly on the toilet, not saying anything. When David saw her reaction, he asked, "What's wrong, honey?"

She told David that she didn't want to be a mommy. He turned and looked straight into her eyes and said, "I don't understand. I thought you'd be happy."

Brigitte told David she didn't want to have a baby because they had only been dating for four months. David became upset and outraged, shouting at Brigitte, "A child is precious. How could you think about giving it up or having an abortion?"

She told David she wanted to be married with a home and a decent place to raise a child. David cursed and told Brigitte she was being selfish and didn't care about his feelings at all. He stormed out the bathroom and went to work.

Over the next several days, they began to argue a lot because Brigitte was trying to raise money to have the abortion. David refused to give her any, saying, "I will not give you money to kill my kid, Brigitte. F**k you."

By this time, David had begun to verbally abuse Brigitte on a day-to-day basis. She became nervous of David and had begun to see a whole other side of him. This was the first time Brigitte began to notice David's inner ways. She was ashamed and embarrassed to call Texas and tell her mother; she remembered how her parents raised her right, and Brigitte didn't know what to do.

Finally, she went to her friend Diane and cried, asking her for advice on the matter.

Diane told Brigitte, "You only have two more weeks to decide what to do about the baby because at six weeks, there will be a heartbeat and a live human being who will be inside of you. So make your decisions soon, honey." She smiled and hugged Brigitte. "That's all I can tell you."

David had grown impatient with Brigitte and took it upon himself to call her mother in Texas. Her mom was shocked and in disbelief because this couldn't be her daughter—pregnant and not married. And if that's not enough, she wanted to have an abortion. Brigitte's mother told David that she would call the house tomorrow and talk directly with Brigitte about the situation.

The following evening, at approximately 6:00 p.m., Brigitte's mother called the house. David answered the phone and said, "Hello?" He then brought the phone to Brigitte.

Brigitte asked, "Who is it?" He shrugged his shoulders. Then Brigitte said, "Hello."

Her mother laid right into her. She fussed and scolded Brigitte, saying, "You should have been more careful and protected yourself. Now you're pregnant and don't want to have this child. You are a grown woman now, and it's time you start acting like one." Her mother continued, "You may not be married, but that's no excuse when it comes to having a child."

Although Brigitte was upset and inexperienced when it came to kids—let alone having one–her mother reassured her that she would fly down to Florida and stay with her as long as she needed her so Brigitte could have all the help she needed with the baby. Brigitte didn't want to upset her mother any more than she already had, but at the end of the day, she knew she would get the support and love from her entire family. Although they were in Texas, she would be all right.

Thus, the planning for her new bundle of joy began.

Chapter 3

The Pregnancy/Raising of the Child

Time was certainly flying by as David and Brigitte prepared for their little one's arrival. Once she began her prenatal care, Brigitte was placed on bed rest, as she was considered a high-risk candidate. Each day, she woke with a sense of purpose, determined to accomplish what needed to be done before the baby arrived.

David leased a two-bedroom condo with a study, and they decided to take the second bedroom and convert it into a nursery. Since Brigitte wasn't sure at first whether she was having a boy or a girl, she decided to decorate the nursery in pale colors—baby blue, pink, mint green, and yellow. The theme was Disney's Mickey and Minnie Babies decor.

David hired two contractors to put up wallpaper in the nursery, complete with borders. In the center of the room stood a white Jenny Lind crib adorned with Mickey-themed decor, including baby sheets, pillows, and blankets. The baby mobile was beautiful as it hung over the crib. There was a white dresser for the baby clothes to go in and a matching changing table.

But there was something missing. Once they put the furniture in the room, David asked Brigitte what else did she think they needed. Brigitte paused and looked around. Then it dawned on her: she would need a rocking chair to feed and nurse the baby.

David said, "Consider it done." He went to a local retail store in Tampa called Montgomery Ward's and visited the baby section. The saleslady asked what David was looking for. He replied, "A rocking chair with a glider for my fiancée." She showed him the available options, including the nursery furniture on display.

All of a sudden, he saw it—the perfect chair. It had a blue padded seat cushion, hand-stitched in an array of colors that kind of matched the wallpaper Brigitte had put up. David was overwhelmed; he purchased it and had it delivered the next day.

Brigitte was overjoyed when it arrived. It was the final piece that made the nursery complete. Over the next several months, Brigitte often found herself going into local stores like Target and Toys "R" Us, heading straight to the baby section to see the newest arrivals in clothing. When Brigitte was six months pregnant, her best friend Nikki called to tell her she was planning a baby shower back home. Because Brigitte lived out of state, Nikki couldn't surprise her with it. She would either have to fly or drive down. Brigitte was thrilled at the chance to experience this with her best friend and family.

So, yup, another road trip was in the making. David and Brigitte took off and headed to Texas. Since she was pregnant, they didn't drive straight through; instead, they stayed overnight in Mississippi and headed to Texas the next morning. They arrived on Friday, with the shower scheduled for Saturday. Brigitte spent time visiting her mother and family, and everyone had a good laugh at how extremely pregnant she looked. Brigitte treated herself to getting her hair done, along with a manicure and pedicure, in preparation for the event.

The next day the baby shower was held at Nikki's mom's house, a large two-story home in DeSoto. Brigitte arrived with David, her hair wrapped and styled in long layers. She wore a two-piece pink short set, perfect for the summer, along with flat black sandals. Although her feet had swollen from riding in the car for two days, she managed to slip them on. As soon as she walked through the front door, she was greeted warmly by everyone—even some of her former college classmates.

Delighted to see everyone, the day was off to a fantastic start. Games came first, of course, and everyone laughed as they played the Clothespin Game. All the appetizers and hors d'oeuvres were prepared, and the cake was decorated in baby blue, because by that time, Brigitte knew she was expecting a boy. All the ladies began fixing their plates while Nikki prepared the gift tables.

By this time, David was in the living room with a few other men when Brigitte noticed something odd—David was flirting with Kathy, an old college friend of hers. At first, she tried to say it was nothing, since Kathy kept everything friendly, but David seemed intent on talking to her throughout the shower. This was the second sign that Brigitte noticed something was off about David's behavior.

As the evening progressed, Brigitte had racked up quite a few baby items, including a car seat and a stroller. She was thrilled, knowing her family was delighted as well—especially her mother, since this was going to be her first grandson.

Sunday morning rolled around, and David was busy loading the car as they were headed back to Florida. Brigitte hugged her mom and promised to call as soon as they arrived home. Her mother waved and said, "I love you guys."

On the road, David asked Brigitte if she had enjoyed herself, and she said yes. Brigitte mentioned Kathy, asking if he had properly introduced himself. David smiled with a slight hesitation and said, "Oh yes."

Brigitte looked at him and said, "You seemed quite cozy with her. She's a friend of mine, and you should respect that."

David then turned to Brigitte and said, "Yes, I will respect that, but it doesn't hurt to look."

That was the third time Brigitte felt something was off about David. After all, they were expecting their first child together. When they finally made it back to Tampa, both exhausted, they managed to get all the baby gifts inside the house.

As the months seemed to fly by, Brigitte prepared for the baby. She and David made sure everything was in place—checking the car seat to ensure it was installed correctly and mapping out the route to the hospital for a mad dash in the middle of the night. They just wanted everything to be perfect.

As Brigitte entered her last trimester, her doctor decided it was time to induce labor due to her swollen feet and the weight she had gained. Dr. Karen told Brigitte she was going to break her water, and after that the contractions would begin. And oh my God, did those contractions start. Brigitte screamed, gripping the rails of her bed tightly, as she never experienced this type of pain. David was there, coaching her, but all she wanted was for the pain to stop.

Although Brigitte had originally wanted to give birth naturally, that was no longer an option. She screamed, "Give me the epidural now!" The first attempt failed—the doctor couldn't hit the nerve. The second time, the needle didn't go in all the way. Finally, they decided to send for a third doctor. By the time he arrived and administered the drug, Brigitte passed out.

Her doctor rushed in, demanding, "What the hell did you do to my patient?" Brigitte was incoherent, she couldn't hold on, and she was fading in and out. Dr. Karen told David, "I'm sorry, but we have to take this baby now. So you're going to have to step out, as we don't have much time."

Dr. Karen performed an emergency C-section on Brigitte as both her blood pressure and the baby's had dropped to an all-time low. Dr. Karen kept shouting, "Brigitte, can you hear me?" Brigitte could hear her but wasn't responding accordingly.

David stood outside the door; he was nervous and scared, and he paced the floor. Soon, a nurse came out and said, "The doctor has made the incision, and I will keep you posted."

Several minutes passed by, and the same nurse returned and said, "Wait a minute—you should hear your son crying." Seconds later, David heard his baby cry for the first time.

Brigitte remained unconscious throughout the delivery and didn't see her baby until hours later. David told her their son was beautiful and healthy. The doctors had taken the baby for some tests to make sure he was in good health.

After a couple of hours, the nurse brought the baby in, and Brigitte got to hold her son for the first time. He was everything Brigitte had imagined—beautiful, with coal-black hair and blue eyes. She cried as she couldn't believe she was finally a mother and David was a father.

Chapter 4

David's Strange Behavior

As the weeks passed, Brigitte stayed busy taking care of her newborn while seeking a full-time job. Although her son, Gabriel, was too cute to leave for even a moment, she knew money would be tight now with the baby. David was the only one working at the time, and Brigitte's mother helped out by sending money to buy the first case of formula, while Brigitte purchased the second case of Similac.

In the evenings, Brigitte began noticing David wasn't coming home right after work. At first, she didn't think anything of it, until she realized he had been gone the entire day—leaving the house around seven-thirty that morning and not returning until after six in the evening. Since Brigitte was a stay-at-home mom, David seemed to feel she could take care of their son all on her own.

Her mornings began around eight-thirty, when she would get Gabriel up, wash his face, change his diapers, prepare his bottles, and feed him. Once Gabriel fell asleep, Brigitte cleaned the nursery and the rest of the house. Her days felt endless with all the chores, and by evening she was desperate for a break.

Brigitte started calling David's office, asking, "When will you be home?" David would reply, "As soon as I get there." His demeanor had begun to change toward Brigitte as well. Suddenly, he wasn't as loving or affectionate toward her. In fact, David started to distance himself from her.

Although she had gained quite a bit of weight during her pregnancy, she knew the importance of regaining her figure and maintaining her looks. Brigitte went on the SlimFast diet and lost an additional twenty-six pounds, on top of the weight she had dropped during her six-day hospital stay on a clear liquid diet. But maybe she thought David didn't find her attractive anymore or sexy; after all, she was a mom, and that took priority over everything else.

Once David was home, he hardly acted as though he was happy to see his child. Brigitte often found herself fussing at him, saying, "You don't want to spend any time with your son. You've been gone all day at work, around coworkers and friends, while I've had to be home all day taking care of Gabriel. You never want to give me a break. David would always tell Brigitte she was overreacting and exaggerating everything.

There were times when David would get home to find Brigitte standing in the doorway with Gabriel. The moment he walked in, she handed him their son and left the house. This seemed to be the only way she could get David to deal with his child.

Often, Brigitte went to Diane and her husband's, Winston's, home. They were the godparents. Brigitte would cry to Diane about how David wasn't helping with their child and behaved as though he didn't want to be around them. Diane would say to Brigitte, "It just takes some time for men to get used to having a baby around." But Brigitte couldn't forget that this was the same man who had cursed her when she had considered abortion. Now that the child was here, David seemed to take a back seat when it came to Gabriel.

One Saturday, David was in his office working on his computer when Brigitte walked in and said, "Now that we're both parents, have you given any thought to locating your biological parents? I'm sure they'd be delighted to find out they have a grandchild."

Brigitte grew up with both her grandparents. When she was little, both she and her brother spent a lot of time over with them during summers and holidays. Brigitte knew how important it was for children to have family around them, to know and love. Since David had hardly any family other than a cousin with two grown children of her own, Brigitte wanted their baby to be exposed to as much family as possible.

David replied calmly, "I don't want to talk about my parents."

Brigitte responded just as calmly, "David, it's important that our son have his grandparents in his life. My family is out of state in Texas, so maybe this could be a good idea if we found your parents."

David then became irritated and slammed his hand on his keyboard and told Brigitte, "I said I didn't want to find those people. Now don't bring that shit up no more because I don't want to fucking hear it. Do you understand me?"

Brigitte stood there, frozen and scared. She didn't open her mouth at all.

David stormed right past her and left the house for the day. This was the fourth red flag that had happened with David. Brigitte began to cry. It became clear to her: she really didn't know David at all. As a matter of fact, she didn't know anything about this man—his family or where he came from. David kept Brigitte completely in the dark about his past. So, every time Brigitte would mention to David about getting familiar with his family, it always ended as an argument and made Brigitte feel terrible.

As the weeks went by, David became more and more distant toward Brigitte and showed less affection. This kind and gentle man that she met just a few months ago was now like a stranger she was living with. Brigitte no longer felt comfortable marrying a man like that. The mysterious side of David puzzled Brigitte and left her uneasy.

She wasn't sure about anything anymore, except for loving her son and taking care of Gabriel which. At times David even seemed jealous of the attention Brigitte gave their child. One day, while she was busy attending to Gabriel and playing with him, David made a comment that pushed her too far.

"All you seem to do is spend time playing with Gabriel instead of me," he said.

Brigitte stood up, looked David straight in the eyes, and replied, "He's a baby. He can't take care of himself. You can, David."

From that point on, Brigitte no longer wanted to be engaged to David. She officially called the wedding off.

David was not Happy at all that Brigitte had called off the wedding. For some strange reason, he believed he had complete control over her and her mindset. But Brigitte was determined to get herself back to work. She knew that having a job and her own money would make her independent again, so she wouldn't have to rely on David for anything.

She signed up with several temp agencies, hoping to get her foot in the door with something temporary that might lead to a permanent position. Finally, Brigitte landed a full-time job working as a debt collector, and she also began looking for a part-time job. By this time, she was concentrating all her efforts on moving out and getting her own place. Money was urgent—she was now a single mom with a small child.

Once Brigitte secured both a full-time and part-time job, she realized she needed a babysitter for Gabriel on weekends. By then he was in daycare, so she asked around to see if any of the teachers were interested in earning extra cash by babysitting on Saturdays. Gabriel was fourteen months old and in the toddler room when his teacher, Ms. Shelia, heard about Brigitte's search. Since she knew both Brigitte and David, she volunteered to take on the job of babysitting Gabriel while Brigitte worked.

Chapter 5

Betrayed/Deceived

The day before Brigitte was to start her new part-time job, she invited Shelia and her daughter, Megan, over to the house so Shelia could get familiar with everything while babysitting Gabriel. On Saturdays, Brigitte drove to Shelia's house to pick her up and bring her over, since Shelia didn't drive. Shelia knew David from the daycare, and David knew of her.

When Brigitte was at work on Saturdays, David and Shelia became quite close. Although Brigitte had called off the wedding and officially ended her relationship with David in January 1999, they were still living under the same roof. Out of respect, Brigitte never dated anyone else, as her priority was working and saving as much money as she could. David and Brigitte were no longer intimate, but David seemed determined to satisfy his needs elsewhere—and what better way to hurt Brigitte than by sleeping with her friend Shelia. Angered that Brigitte called off the wedding, David saw this as payback.

The two began an affair, both knowing that if Brigitte found out, it would end badly. Brigitte would terminate her friendship with Shelia, never allow her near Gabriel again, and immediately move out of David's house. Even though they were no longer together, David enjoyed the fact that Brigitte still lived in his home, as it allowed him to know her whereabouts at all times.

David told Shelia, "We can never let Brigitte find out. We have to keep this between us." She went along with it, hoping that eventually she and David could start a serious relationship, as she was divorced.

After four months of saving, Brigitte was finally ready to move out. She found a charming townhouse just down the street from David's, in a quiet neighborhood with a beautiful pond behind the complex. It had two bedrooms, two full baths, and a half bath downstairs. She told the landlord she had a small child, and the unit would be perfect for them. They agreed, and the landlord told Brigitte the deposit would be $700 plus the first month's rent. Brigitte had the money and signed the lease.

Finally, the day came for Brigitte to move. Although she had told David several times, he never believed she would actually do it. He often said to her, "No man will want to be with you. You have a small child, and you're unmarried. No guy is going to want that responsibility." The verbal abuse Brigitte endured from David was mortifying, as it never seemed to stop. The very idea of escaping both David and his cruelty made her happy.

The movers arrived, and the day was filled with excitement. Boxes were being taped up, furniture was carried out, and everything was loaded onto the truck. Brigitte wrapped dishes carefully, eager to settle into her new place. Everyone was doing their part. The movers were lifting Brigitte's couch when David suddenly came home. Outraged by the scene, he yelled, "What's the meaning of this?"

Brigitte turned to him with a slight smirk and said, "I'm moving out today."

Flabbergasted, David couldn't believe his eyes. He told Brigitte, "You didn't tell me you were moving out today."

She replied, "I've been saying it for the past six months." Although David knew Brigitte was telling the truth, he never imagined it would actually happen.

When the affair between David and Shelia began, of course Brigitte didn't know about it. But she remembered back when they first met—David had been a player and loved having women in his life. Shortly thereafter, David moved a young lady named Michelle into his house. She and David were supposedly involved in a serious relationship.

Brigitte had always told David she had no problem with their son around his girlfriends, but Brigitte needed to meet them first so she could feel comfortable knowing who they were. At first, David procrastinated, always making excuses that he and Michelle were busy or going out. Brigitte said okay, until one day she took it upon herself to drive over to David's house and knock on the door.

David came downstairs to answer. Brigitte said, "Well, I'm here—so let's meet Michelle since you've had my son around her, and I don't know who she is."

Michelle came downstairs to meet Brigitte. Brigitte introduced herself and said, "I just needed to meet you. Since you're going to be around my child, I wanted to put a face with a name." They both seemed to have a mutual respect for each other, and afterward Brigitte left.

Over the next several weekends, Shelia continued babysitting Gabriel for Brigitte, but now she did so at Brigitte's house instead of David's. One particular day, Michelle called Brigitte, crying and upset. She told Brigitte that another woman called on the phone and told Michelle that she was David's girlfriend. Michelle, who was Spanish, explained that the woman had a Spanish accent as well.

Michelle asked Brigitte if she knew anyone like that. Not wanting to get involved in David's affairs, Brigitte said no. But she knew Shelia was the only other person with a Spanish accent because she was from Puerto Rico. Brigitte told Michelle that although she didn't get involved with David's personal business, he was known for being a womanizer and for having multiple ladies in his life. She warned Michelle to be careful if she planned to stay with him.

Once Brigitte hung up the phone, she was livid. How could Shelia and David betray her like that? She had trusted them both, and now the truth about their love affair and sexual relationship was out.

Brigitte called a friend from work, a girl named Denise, and told her everything Michelle had said. Brigitte asked Denise what she should do. Denise replied, "Confront Shelia. Call her on the phone, tell her what Michelle told you, and then ask, 'Are you sleeping with David?' Listen carefully to what she says and how she responds. Her voice and demeanor will tell you everything—but mostly, it will let you know if she's lying or telling the truth."

So Brigitte called Shelia and asked her point-blank if she was sleeping with David behind her back.

Shelia responded vaguely and nervously, saying, "Oh no, Mami. I would never do anything like that. You are my friend—I wouldn't hurt you like that." Although Shelia sounded sincere, Brigitte knew she was lying. From that moment on, she realized she could never trust her again.

Shortly thereafter, Brigitte quit her part-time job, as she could now manage on her full-time salary. She no longer needed Shelia to babysit her son. By then Gabriel was in the two-year-old classroom at the daycare center, which meant Brigitte hardly had to see Shelia anymore. In her mind, once a liar, always a liar.

Chapter 6

Brigitte Gets Engaged

It had been four months since Brigitte began living on her own with her son. She never seriously considered dating anyone—being a single mom and working full-time kept her busy enough. She did have one friend she met through the personal ads, a local man from Tampa named Randy. He had a great sense of humor and knew Brigitte had a small child, but he didn't mind that so much, as he had no children of his own. Although they went out on several dates, Brigitte knew she couldn't get too serious with Randy. He was married, though separated from his wife for two years. She told herself there was no real future there.

Back in Texas, Brigitte had a lot of friends—people she had gone to high school and college with, as well as sisters from her sorority, Zeta Phi Beta. But there was one particular gentleman she had met when she was seventeen, through a mutual friend. His name was Copeland. He was twelve years older than Brigitte but knew her family well.

Her parents met him one Saturday at her father's insistence. Since Brigitte was still in high school and underage, her father felt it was best to lay down some ground rules with Copeland, as Brigitte was his youngest daughter. Her parents allowed them to court with the understanding that Brigitte had a curfew and had to be home by

10:00 p.m. on weekends—and absolutely no sex, as she was a minor. Her father told Copeland.

Being a respectful guy, Copeland honored Brigitte's father's request and only casually dated her. He took her shopping, out to dinner, and to the movies—anything Brigitte enjoyed doing. At 10:00 p.m. on the dot, Copeland always had Brigitte home, just as her father instructed. Brigitte believed her dad had simply scared Copeland to death when it came to her.

Once Brigitte graduated from high school and went off to college, she and Copeland kept in touch. He still made an effort to see her whenever she came home, as he worked for a local company in Dallas as a long-distance driver. When Brigitte eventually moved out of state, it became tough for Copeland to see her, but they managed to write to and call each other whenever they had the opportunity.

Once Brigitte moved to Tampa and became involved with David, she didn't talk to Copeland nearly as much. She was dating someone else now. Still, Copeland would phone her occasionally, and if David wasn't around, Brigitte would chat with him.

When Brigitte became pregnant and had Gabriel, she didn't tell Copeland right away. They had been friends for nine years, and she felt that out of respect he had the right to know. But she wanted to tell him in person, not in a letter or over the phone.

So naturally, when Brigitte moved out of David's house, she reached out to Copeland and invited him to visit when he had the chance. Copeland accepted her offer and requested a week off from his job to come down to Florida. She was excited but also nervous— Copeland didn't know about Gabriel, as she had kept that a secret. Although she had told him she needed to speak with him about something, she still felt awkward. Copeland, in turn, said he needed to talk to her as well.

It was Friday, and after getting off work, Brigitte went straight home and busied herself cleaning, knowing Copeland would arrive the next day. She didn't know what to expect or how he would react once he learned about her son. Seeking advice, she called Diane, Gabriel's godmother, and told her what was going on. Diane told Brigitte, "Tell Copeland the moment you pick him up from the bus station. Let him know you're a mother now, and that Gabriel and you come as a package deal. If that's too much for him, he can go back to Texas—because Gabriel is here to stay."

Brigitte took Diane's advice. When she picked up Copeland and they got into the car, Brigitte turned and told him, "I need to tell you something." She was anxious and nervous. She finally told him, "I have a child now, and his name is Gabriel. He's two years old."

Copeland looked at her, smiled, and said, "You're a mommy now, Brigitte."

She nodded. "Yes, I'm a mother."

Copeland hugged her tightly and said, "I'm so happy for you. I can't wait to meet your son."

Shock and surprised, Brigitte couldn't believe how Copeland was being so nice about it.

They took off and headed toward Brigitte's house. Once they got home, Copeland took his bags upstairs and said he wanted to take Brigitte out to dinner.

The next morning, David brought Gabriel home to Brigitte. She was already up as Copeland was taking a shower upstairs. When he got dressed, he came down, and Brigitte was holding Gabriel. "Copeland, this is my son," she said.

Copeland's eyes filled with joy. "He's beautiful—he looks just like you," he told her. Brigitte set Gabriel down and said, "This is Mommy's friend Copeland."

Gabriel walked over to him, and Copeland picked him up and said, "Hi, buddy" and gave him a hug.

Afterward, he put Gabriel down and said, "Can you help me with something?"

Gabriel, now talking, replied, "Okay." Brigitte sat on the couch as Copeland reached into his pocket, pulled out a small box, and handed it to Gabriel. "Take this to Mommy," he said.

Gabriel carried it over and said, "Mommy, this is for you."

Brigitte's eyes grew wide, and she started tearing up. Copeland came over, got down on one knee, and said, "Brigitte, I know we've known each other for a long time and that we've both been living separate lives, but I have never stopped caring about you—or loving you. I want to help you raise Gabriel, if you'll let me, Brigitte. He paused before asking, "Will you marry me?"

Completely overwhelmed, Brigitte threw her arms around him and cried, "Yes! Yes, Copeland, I will marry you."

And so it began—Copeland and Brigitte were now officially engaged to be married.

Chapter 7

Transitioning Back Home

Once Brigitte accepted Copeland's proposal, she knew David wouldn't be happy at all when he got wind of the news. Brigitte had told David about Copeland, explaining that they had been long-term friends from years ago. But friendship was one thing—this man had not only swooped into town and won Brigitte's heart, but also he was now going to become her husband. That meant another male figure in Gabriel's life, someone the boy might one day call "Daddy."

Brigitte knew this wouldn't go over well, especially with her plans to relocate back to Texas. Still, her mind was made up—she was going home to marry Copeland, no matter what.

At first, she thought of an excuse David might easily believe. One day she called him and said she had decided to move back home to look after her mother. After all, it had been Brigitte's older sister who had taken on the role of caregiver, and now Brigitte felt it was her turn to give her sister a break.

But David wasn't entirely convinced. He insisted they meet to talk about their son, Gabriel, and to work out visitation arrangements. In Brigitte's mind, she suspected something was going down. Why would David need to meet up with her?

Brigitte didn't wear her engagement ring. It was David who suggested that Brigitte let him keep Gabriel with him in Tampa until she had settled in with her sister, found a job, and arranged proper daycare in Texas. "Once you've established those parameters," he told her, "I will bring Gabriel to you in Texas."

At first, the idea seemed reasonable. It would give Brigitte the opportunity to get herself together and take care of things once she returned home. So Brigitte agreed. She put in her two weeks' notice at work and began boxing up her belongings, ready to be move. This would make her third move. She hired some movers and reserve a U-Haul truck with a car dolly.

Jeremiah, her mother's boyfriend, came down to help with the move. Brigitte and Jeremiah had a great rapport; he had been there for her mother when she needed a friend. After Brigitte's father passed away, Jeremiah grew very close to the family.

They set off on the long trip, but they always made the best of it—stopping for burgers and fries, drinking sodas, listening to music, and enjoying themselves on the highway. Finally, they arrived in Texas.

Although Brigitte was engaged, she wanted to honor her family traditions by not living with a man until marriage. After all, she didn't want to make the same mistake she made with David. Copeland understood and respected her wishes.

Her mother and sister were standing outside, waiting, when they pulled up. All the excitement was in the air as her mom was delighted that both her daughters would be living under the same roof with her. They could be a family again. Jeremiah got Brigitte's car off the car dolly and began unloading boxes into the garage. Brigitte had rented a large storage unit for the rest of her furniture until she found her own place. It was a good day—being back in her native state, surrounded by the man she loved and her family.

But behind closed doors, David was making plans of his own—plans Brigitte was completely unaware of. He intended to keep her in the dark until the time came to strike back.

Once home, Brigitte phoned Tampa to let David know she had arrived safely. She asked how Gabriel was doing. David replied, "He's fine." She then asked to speak to her son. Gabriel said, "Mommy, I miss you."

Brigitte told him, "It's just for a little while, son. Daddy will bring you to live with me. So be a good boy, and Mommy will see you soon."

Brigitte hit the ground running, looking for full-time work. She signed up with local temp agencies and took whatever assignments she could until she landed something permanent. She worked during the day and spent her evenings at home with her mom. Copeland would come over, and together they would sit and have dinner together.

Copeland and Brigitte were so happy to finally be together, though they hadn't taken the time to actually set a wedding date yet with all the changes in their lives. Finally, Brigitte landed a full-time job working as an insurance follow-up claim representative for a medical billing company specializing in oncology patients. It was a very demanding job, as Brigitte was responsible for the accounts receivable side of patient billing and ensuring physicians were paid for the services they provided. Each passing day, Brigitte missed her son, but she always called during the week to check on Gabriel.

After being home for a month and finding two suitable daycare centers, Brigitte began to ask David, "When are you planning on bringing Gabriel out to Texas? I'm working full-time now, and I have found two daycare centers near my job."

David would always reply using his cold and malicious voice, "I will bring him when I'm ready to bring him. You don't have to keep asking me that, Brigitte."

By this time, David had somehow found out that Brigitte was engaged and he was livid that she lied to him about her move. David had no intention on letting Brigitte move to Texas and live happily ever after. He was determined to wreck all her plans of getting married to another man.

Finally, after about seven weeks David was ready. He called Brigitte and told her he was driving Gabriel down to Texas. Brigitte was super excited to finally have her little man back home with her, not knowing David had his plans in the making.

He told her they should arrive there by Saturday. Friday came, and Brigitte was anxious. She finished up at work and rushed home to make sure the house was ready, as her sister had a two-story home with three bedrooms and a loft upstairs. Gabriel was going to share a bedroom with Brigitte so everyone would have their own room.

Saturday morning came and Brigitte and her sister were up making sure the house was clean, the laundry done, and that there was plenty of food in the fridge. The afternoon rolled around, and Brigitte and her sister Yolanda sat at the table playing a card game (Spade) when her sister looked out the living room window and saw this huge U-Haul truck outside. Puzzled, Yolanda said she wasn't expecting anyone but it was only David. She assumed he'd be in a car.

Yolanda told Brigitte to go look outside. Brigitte asked why. Her sister said, "I think you need to see what's going on."

Brigitte went outside and saw the truck. At first, she thought someone lost their way or had the wrong house. But as Brigitte walked toward the truck, the door opened and David came out, staring at her.

She asked, "What is this truck doing here? I thought you were bringing Gabriel and going back to Tampa. Why is this U-Haul truck here at my sister's home?"

David then replied, "I've decided to move here so that I can be closer to my son."

At that moment, Brigitte was outraged. She told David, "You didn't move here to be closer to your son. You moved here because I'm here. Your son has nothing to do with this."

David had stalked Brigitte across four state lines, all the way to Texas. Now Brigitte's worst nightmare had begun. Brigitte then asked David, "Where are you planning on staying?"

He replied, "I don't have any money, so I was going to ask your sister if I could live here with you all until I get my own apartment."

Brigitte was angry. She said, "There's no way you don't have money. You're in money markets, so making money is what you do best. Besides, you shouldn't have moved if your finances didn't allow it. Moving into my sister's home is wrong and disrespectful. There's no extra room for you here, so you need to find some other place to stay."

David looked at Brigitte and said, "This isn't your house."

She then replied, "It's my sister's home."

So he walked inside the house, and before Brigitte could give her sister "that look" to say no, David went in for the kill. He told Yolanda that he was sorry for imposing on her like this, but he moved to Texas because "as a father, I want to be close to my son, but I don't have any money right now to get my own place. If I give you $500 cash today and pay that to you monthly, could I live here just for a little while until I get my own place? As a mother of two daughters, I'm sure you know the importance of being close to your kids."

By that time, Brigitte sat there with envy and thought, *You SOB. How dare you use my nieces to gain favor with my sister.*

Yolanda told David, "I only have a loft area upstairs. The couch pulls out into a sofa bed, and there's a bathroom upstairs."

David smiled and said, "That's perfect." Then he looked at Brigitte with a smirk, as if to say, Now let the games begin.

David's whole idea was to get back under the same roof as Brigitte so he could keep up with her daily. He used Shelia the babysitter in Tampa when he wanted to know about Brigitte and everything she was doing and who she was seeing—and possibly sleeping with. Shelia betrayed Brigitte and was too stupid enough to see that David was only using her to stay connected to his son's mother.

She told David all of Brigitte's business, and at the end of the day, David didn't want to be with Shelia. So now he needed a new source or a new way of keeping up with Brigitte in every way possible. Living with her sister gave him plenty of access to Brigitte.

Shortly thereafter, Brigitte's mom had been approved for her assisted living apartment in Dallas, and she was quite ready to move in so she could be around people more her age. After she moved out, David took Brigitte's mom's room, which was right next to Brigitte's room.

And just as Brigitte feared, the fussing and arguing began afterward. Once David moved to Texas and knew Brigitte had gotten engaged, he wanted to make things as hard for her as possible. Brigitte would drop off their son at daycare and go on to work. Once the evening rolled around and David had to pick up Gabriel, he would call Brigitte at work and tell her he couldn't get Gabriel. Naturally, Brigitte would have to rush from work, driving fast to get Gabriel picked up before the daycare center closes and she be charged a fee for being late.

On the weekends, when it was David's turn to get Gabriel, he would make up some excuse, like saying he's got to go into the office so Brigitte would have to deal with Gabriel after having him all week long. Luckily, Copeland was off on the weekends as well, so he would tell Brigitte to come over and they would take Gabriel with them. Copeland told Brigitte, "Since I get off at three in the afternoon, I can pick up Gabriel from daycare. That way, you don't have to rush trying to get him picked up."

When David didn't follow through with his responsibilities toward his son, Copeland always came through for Brigitte. David despised Copeland because he knew that he was no competition. The more David tried to complicate things, the more Copeland stepped up to help with Gabriel.

After living with her sister for three months, Brigitte started looking for her own place, as she didn't want to overstay her welcome. Copeland was staying at his mom's house and looking after her since she had suffered a partial stroke on her left side. When he wasn't working, he was spending time with Brigitte and Gabriel and taking care of his mom.

Both Brigitte and Copeland pulled together when it came to getting things done. And that was something that made David have a grudge against both of them. David's overall thoughts consumed with causing problems and dismay for Brigitte—hoping that eventually, Copeland would grow weary and leave her forever.

Chapter 8

Brigitte Gets Married

It was spring 2001, and Brigitte had been living with her sister for about three months. She felt it was time to move into her own place, though her sister didn't mind her staying. Brigitte always wanted Gabriel to have his own room so he wouldn't get comfortable with sleeping in hers, especially since Brigitte was getting married soon. So she found an apartment complex in the Dallas area, about thirty minutes from her job, with Gabriel's daycare located fifteen minutes from the apartment.

Brigitte went ahead and moved out. As always, she got an apartment on the second floor with two bedrooms and two baths so her son could have his own room again. Once she settled in, David soon left her sister's house as well, since it wasn't doing him any good living there after Brigitte had gone. David insisted that Brigitte let him know where she lived since Gabriel would be living with her. Brigitte never had a problem letting David know where she lived; she wanted her son in his father's life.

However, David decided to move across town, nearly an hour away. When Brigitte asked, "Why did you move so far? Are you going to be able to get your son on your weekends?" David's attitude and demeanor had already turned cold and disrespectful. Each time he called the house or spoke to Brigitte in person, he carried an unspoken hatred toward her that made her feel deeply uncomfortable.

Once David returned to work in Dallas, where he was employed in sales, Brigitte often came home to find fifty or fifty calls on her Caller ID from various businesses. She suspected David had put her number on the internet telemarketer to call her house and harass her. Some nights, when it was late, Brigitte would hear knocks at her door while she lived alone with Gabriel. David had become obsessed with her. He wanted her to feel unsafe and scared in her own home. He wanted Brigitte to suffer.

David's tactics grew worse as time went by. One night, he and Brigitte got into an argument, and David called the police on her, claiming he feared his son's life was in danger. The cops came to Brigitte's house that night and asked if everything was all right. She answered yes and explained that she and David had argued but that things were fine now. The police asked to check on Gabriel, and Brigitte took them to his room, where he was sound asleep. The police advised her to document everything and wished her a good night.

From the moment on, Brigitte began keeping records so she would have a paper trail of all the events and everything David had done. He was always using scare tactics to intimidate and frighten her into doing what he wanted. Whenever Brigitte tried to stand her ground, David grew increasingly irate. One reason was that he no longer had access to her—he couldn't see her or listen to her conversations like before when she lived at her sister's home. Cut off and denied access, he became more furious. He wanted Brigitte to be miserable because she had moved on with her life, and he hadn't.

As the months passed, Copeland's mother suffered a second stroke and passed away. It was a devastating blow to everyone who knew her. With that loss and everything else David was doing, both Copeland and Brigitte decided to get married at the courthouse and plan a larger wedding ceremony once things calmed down.

Copeland and Brigitte tied the knot in July 2001. Shortly thereafter, Brigitte moved into Copeland's mother's house while they waited for their new home to be built. Copeland wanted to make sure he took excellent care of his new wife and his stepson, Gabriel. They all were happy, and Brigitte was delighted to finally be a married woman. But little did she know, something terrible was coming her way.

When David heard that Brigitte had married, he went ballistic. His biggest fear had finally come true: the woman he loved—the mother of his child—was now someone else's wife and lover. David knew his chances of ever getting Brigitte back was over. It was never going to happen. She belonged to another man legally, and there was absolutely nothing he could do. Brigitte was out of his life for good, and whatever hopes or plans he may have had were destroyed because she had married another. With Gabriel now having a strong father figure under the same roof, David decided he would not allow Brigitte to go free and be happy. He had no interest in co-parenting or co-existing with her.

The only way he could remotely cause issues for Brigitte was through their son, who was three years old at the time. And that's exactly what David did.

Chapter 9

The Custody Battle

When Brigitte moved out of David's home, he agreed to pay her $400 a month in child support. That was the agreement. But as time went on. Brigitte covered all of Gabriel's expenses—clothes, shoes, haircuts every two weeks, and everything in between. Suddenly, $400 wasn't enough to cover much of anything, especially since Gabriel's daycare cost $150 a week.

So one day at work, Brigitte began talking with a coworker about the rising costs of raising a small child. The coworker told Brigitte that she could consider putting David on formal child support if she felt he wasn't helping or contributing enough. She explained how to file a case with the attorney general's office and what documents Brigitte would need. Brigitte thanked her for everything.

Later on, Keisha—the coworker—invited Brigitte and Gabriel to her church for Sunday morning service. Keisha also mentioned that the church offered children's programs. Brigitte had been raised in the church, so naturally she wanted the same for her son. That following Sunday, she dressed both herself and Gabriel for service, and off they went.

The church was Rogers Baptist Church, just as Keisha had told her. They arrived early enough for Gabriel to attend children's church, while Brigitte sat with Keisha and her family. Afterward, Brigitte and

Keisha went to pick up the children, as Keisha had a young daughter at the time. That was when Brigitte and Gabriel got to meet her daughter, Addison.

Later that evening, Brigitte debated calling David to ask for more financial help with Gabriel. She knew it would likely spark an argument, but she didn't care. This was their son, and everything was becoming so costly for kids. She just needed a little more help.

Brigitte called, and David answered the phone. Right away, she could tell he had an attitude. Brigitte could detect it in his voice. She began to explain how quickly Gabriel was outgrowing his clothes and how, since moving to Texas, she now had to prepare for four seasons. In Florida it was mostly hot year-round, and she hadn't needed to buy winter clothes, but Texas was a different story. She asked David if he could give her a little more each month because the cost of clothing was expensive and daycare fees were high as well.

David couldn't wait to lash out. He used every opportunity to belittle and curse Brigitte. He told her he wasn't going to give her anything extra—that $400 was it, and she would continue receiving it on the nineteenth of each month. Brigitte tried to explain that Gabriel's daycare fees were due every Monday, so by the time she received the child support, the money was already spent. David didn't budge at all. He told her, "You're married. You and your husband should be able to take care of Gabriel."

Brigitte quickly replied, "But Gabriel isn't my husband's son. He's your son, and you have an obligation to help with him."

David hung up the phone and didn't call her back. The following week, she decided to contact the child support office and open a case against him. Once David was notified by the attorney general's office that a case had been opened, he went berserk. He decided to countersue

Brigitte in family court, claiming she was an unfit mother for their son. Brigitte now had to hire a family attorney to fight David in court.

By this time, Gabriel had begun acting out at daycare. Not only was Brigitte dealing with David in court, but now her son was being kicked out of daycare for behavior problems. It was suggested to Brigitte that her son might have ADHD and that therapy could help determine if that was truly the case.

It was hard because Brigitte needed to work—she and her husband had just bought a new house, and she had to keep her job. David's health insurance didn't cover therapy, so Brigitte and her husband paid privately out of pocket. The sessions were costly, and David didn't offer to contribute. By the time they returned to court, David owed Brigitte $800. Yet he sued Brigitte, claiming she was unfit. In reality, it was David who appeared unfit, since he refused to pay for their son's therapy. Brigitte's attorney argued that point in court.

Visitation was established: David would have Gabriel on Wednesday nights, with Brigitte agreeing to let him stay overnight, provided David returned him to daycare the following morning. He also got every other weekend, Father's Day, the entire month of July, and alternating holidays with Brigitte.

It seemed that every time Gabriel returned from David's house, he was out of control. He had begun to act out, but Brigitte refused to tolerate it. She immediately got him back on track, telling him, "That's not happening here at Mommy's house." When Gabriel didn't comply, Brigitte withheld playtime, television, video games, and outside activities. She didn't believe in rewarding bad behavior, so Gabriel quickly learned that Mommy wasn't the one to play with.

By this time, David had become so belligerent during the exchange of their son that Brigitte no longer wanted him coming to their house. She asked her attorney to arrange for them to meet in a public setting instead, because of David's hostile behavior. When David phoned the house and asked for Brigitte, it seemed he only wanted to pick a fight over something trivial. He never asked about his son or how Gabriel was doing; instead, he cursed and insulted Brigitte, calling her the worst names, B—— and H——. Naturally, she hung up the phone because she couldn't tolerate his verbal abuse.

It seemed like the more she tried to set boundaries and raise Gabriel in a two-parent, churchgoing home—with her mother acting as a true asset and wonderful grandmother—the more David seemed determined to tear it down. He didn't care about his son; this was personal. He was going to use Gabriel to lash out and keep Brigitte distracted, even to the point of jeopardizing her work.

Luckily, Brigitte was able to find a local home daycare operated by a woman named Mrs. Mary. Brigitte was desperate, and she explained that she needed to work and, with the custody battle ongoing, she had no choice. Mary knew Gabriel was in play therapy and agreed to take him in until the therapist could determine what was going on. Eventually, Gabriel was diagnosed with ADHD, and the therapist recommended a follow-up with a neurologist to prescribe medication.

In the midst of therapy and now with a neurologist involved, Brigitte and Copeland stayed focused. It was extremely important to Brigitte that she kept her family in church and surrounded by loved ones for support. By this time, David wasn't assisting at all with their son. It appeared he only wanted to cause drama in Brigitte's life, never offering any kind of help, even though he owed outstanding medical expenses for Gabriel.

Initially, Gabriel had been on David's health insurance. But after Brigitte got married, Copeland told her, "Let's put Gabriel on my health insurance. It will cut down some of these costs and bills." That's what they did, and the neurologist's visits were covered at 100 percent, as were Gabriel's medications. This was a blessing—finally, one less thing for Brigitte to worry about when it came to her son.

Brigitte's mother moved in for a short time to help with Gabriel, and she loved being around him every day. Gabriel, in turn, loved having his grandmother living with them, as he got all her attention.

Once David heard about it, he realized Brigitte had a winning support team in her family—something he didn't have. After Gabriel began his medication, Brigitte enrolled him in the school the previous director had recommended, called For Kids Only. She contacted the director, a woman named Gail, and scheduled an appointment to meet her in person and tour the school.

Inside, Brigitte was amazed by the way Gail had set everything up. The classrooms were small, allowing the children plenty of one-on-one time with their teachers. The school had a gym the size of a football field, where the kids had P.E., and an outdoor play area that resembled the Play Zone Center, filled with equipment any child would love. The menu was provided through an accredited food program, and the curriculum followed that of Garland ISD, a prestigious school district in the Garland suburbs.

Brigitte was overjoyed. She knew this was the best school for Gabriel. She explained to Gail all that had transpired with her son— that he was now on medication, had completed therapy, and just needed another chance at being a kid again. Gail graciously accepted Gabriel into the program and was delighted to work with Brigitte to help him get back on track.

It had been a long journey these past six months with Gabriel, but all the hard work and effort had paid off. Brigitte was excited that her son was doing well, and she hoped David would share the same enthusiasm. But he didn't. Instead, he was determined to cause trouble at this daycare, just as he had at the previous ones, hoping Gail—the director—would disenroll Gabriel and leave Brigitte in another difficult situation. But thanks be to God, Gail was not easily bullied or pushed around by David.

On several occasions, David argued with the staff, demanding that they provide him with Gabriel's medication to take home. The staff refused, explaining that the medication was for Gabriel and would remain at the school so it could be administered when he arrived. David became upset, screaming and yelling, and causing a scene. Finally, Gail banned him from the property altogether. She made it clear that if David set one foot on her grounds, she would have him arrested for trespassing.

Everywhere David went, when it came to his son, he caused trouble and created scenes. Though he was an educated man with both a bachelor's and a master's degree, his behavior resembled that of a thug or hoodlum rather than someone with higher education.

Now that David was banned from Gabriel's school and no longer allowed to pick him up, he called Brigitte and said, "You're going to have to bring my son to me since I can't pick him up."

She responded, "That's not my fault—you got yourself banned from the school."

David went on to tell Brigitte that if he didn't see his son or that if she didn't bring him to David, he was going to take her back to court and say that she refused to let him see his child. He hoped she would be found in contempt for violating the court order.

As a result, Brigitte and her attorney had to make arrangements outside of court to ensure she could bring Gabriel to David.

Since Brigitte's marriage to Copeland was complete and David displayed such hostility toward her husband, she no longer wanted him coming to their house. Instead, they agreed to meet at a local library to exchange their son—another added responsibility David placed on Brigitte.

Throughout the three years of the custody battle, David seemed to get away with everything. The family courts of Dallas, Texas, felt far too lenient to Brigitte, as they never held him accountable or punished him for failing to comply with the very court order he had typed up. She often wondered if his being Caucasian played a role in the way he was given a slap on the wrist, while she was held to the strictest standard when it came to obeying the court's order.

David dragged the case out for a long time. Financially, it became a heavy strain on Brigitte and her husband, who had to keep an attorney on retainer. David filed motion after motion, knowing it would wear Brigitte down physically and mentally. Each time they reached an agreement on visitation or any other matter, and just as the final court order was about to be signed, David would pull a last-minute stunt, and the process would begin all over again. He lived for this, and his conduct was unbecoming. He had become a madman, clearly out to destroy Brigitte no matter what.

One day, during an exchange of their son, David told Brigitte to her face, "I will continue to spend your husband's money until you go broke, file for bankruptcy, or lose your home." At that moment, Brigitte realized she couldn't escape David's treacherous ways. No matter how responsible she was with Gabriel, she now understood this was personal—it was never about their child. This was David's way of punishing her for leaving him, moving on, and getting married.

Brigitte told her mother she didn't even want child support from David. If she had known it would cause this much trouble, she said, she would never have filed. Brigitte felt trapped, knew for certain David was coming for blood, and there was no way she could escape the hell he was putting her through.

Chapter 10

Brigitte Fights Back

Once Gabriel was enrolled in Gail's school, the medication he was taking helped him stay focused in class for maybe six or seven hours. By the time Brigitte arrived to pick him up, however, the effects had worn off and Gabriel was full of energy again. One of the teachers suggested that Brigitte consider putting Gabriel in an extracurricular activity to help contain his energy and, at same time, give him a healthy outlet.

At that point, Brigitte said she would start looking into it as she thought, Gabriel, now four years old, was ready. She believed that joining a little league football or soccer team could help him develop, engage with children his age, and learn to coexist as part of a team. As the custodial parent, and with Gabriel living with her and her husband, she made all the decision regarding him. In the past, she had tried to include David in parenting matters, but he never showed interest. He often dismissed her ideas, saying things like, "You're always looking for ways to spend money or make extra bills," never recognizing the benefits or sacrifices Gabriel could gain from such experiences. Naturally, Brigitte discussed these matters with Copeland or her mother instead.

As the months passed, Brigitte continued transporting Gabriel to the library for exchanges, since David had officially been banned from his school. Of course, David never offered Brigitte gas money for bringing his son to him since he knew she was tired. Sometimes Copeland would take Gabriel to meet David to give Brigitte a break or let her sleep in on Saturday mornings after a long week.

When Gabriel spent weekends with David, it gave Brigitte and Copeland some quality time together. Yet she often regretted it, knowing that when she picked Gabriel up, he would be out of control and she would have to get him back on track. She didn't tolerate bad behavior. Often, she preferred having Gabriel at home with them rather than at his father's house.

In January 2003, Brigitte finally decided to enroll Gabriel in an activity. She enrolled him into tae kwon do. After doing a little research, she discovered that this activity taught children self-respect, discipline, and how to be team players. Gabriel was very excited about the idea of attending martial arts classes and wearing his uniform. On Saturdays, Brigitte and Copeland came out to watch the events and see Gabriel perform. They were proud of their son and knew he was doing well. Everything seemed perfect—until David decided to join the class.

On Tuesdays, Brigitte took Gabriel to practice. When she walked inside, she immediately saw David in practice with the children. Brigitte nearly collapsed from shock. Her first thought was *What in the hell are you doing here with these children? David knew Brigitte bought Gabriel to practice, and whenever he learned of an event or suspected she would be present, he took advantage of the opportunity. He was determined to make Brigitte see him, no matter what he had to do.*

By this time, the stalking was as real as it could get. Joining the class was the perfect front—not because David was interested in Gabriel, but because he wanted to see Brigitte. He had become completely obsessed, harassing, tormenting, and badgering her at every chance. To Brigitte, it seemed David had developed a game strategy for the custody battle, using it to keep her under his control with his sadistic behavior. He had no intention of getting along with her. Instead, he was determined to manipulate and scare her into doing what he wanted. Each time she refused or stood against him, he pulled another stunt.

Brigitte reached the point where she no longer wanted any contact with David. She knew he had the upper hand and that no matter how much she jumped through his hoops and hurdles, it was never going to be enough. David played the family courts to his favor, manipulating everyone into believing he was interested in co-parenting with Brigitte. But that, in itself, was a lie.

It was February 3, 2003—a typical Saturday, or at least that's how it began. Gabriel had a tae kwon do competition that day. Brigitte and her husband got up early to cook breakfast and get Gabriel fed and dressed. The event was scheduled for eleven that morning. They both wanted to get there early to secure good seats to watch him perform. David showed up in his attire as well.

When Gabriel's age group went on first, they all did extremely well. Brigitte was so proud to see her four-year-old son out front, performing his martial arts moves. Tears filled her eyes as she thought of how far he had come—overcoming obstacles and finally enjoying himself, simply being a kid again.

The competition ended around one that afternoon. Parents went down to the floor to congratulate their children on a job well done. Brigitte and Copeland walked outside with Gabriel when David approached and said, "I'm taking Gabriel home with me."

Brigitte responded, "But it's not your weekend to have him— it's mine."

David stood there and looked Brigitte in the eyes. He said, "Look, bitch, you can't fucking tell me when I can or can't spend any extra time with my kid. If you try to, I will fucking kill you."

At that exact moment, all the hurt, frustration, lies, and betrayal Brigitte had endured surged within her. She felt all her anger rising, and the shit David had put her through was just too damn much. The adrenaline cursed through her body, and all she saw was red. Brigitte picked up a wooden board and swung at David. She thought to herself, *If you're going to kill me, I'm not going down without a fight.*

The altercation lasted about fifteen minutes before the police arrived. Brigitte was arrested and charged with aggravated assault with a deadly weapon. Copeland was also taken into custody for unpaid tickets his employer had failed to cover. That's how David ended up with Gabriel in his custody.

Copeland was released later that day after a friend came down and paid the tickets on his behalf. Brigitte, however, had to remain in jail over the weekend. Since she had used a weapon to assault David, she had to be arraigned and appear before a judge on Monday to have her bail set.

Once Monday came, Brigitte stood before the judge, and her bail was set at $50,000. Her husband needed to raise 5 percent to secure her release from jail. Meanwhile, David rushed to family court, requesting an emergency hearing to change custody, believing Brigitte was going to be in jail for a while. But Brigitte was released on bond, and her attorney immediately called to inform her they had to be in court the next morning. Brigitte barely had time to get home and take a bath after being locked up.

Prior to this incident, Brigitte had won the custody battle against David, but now he knew the courts would give him Gabriel.

Luckily, the same judge presided over their case, which was an advantage for Brigitte and her attorney, since the judge already knew the facts from the beginning. Judge Harries was aware of Brigitte's criminal case and the restraining order David had obtained against her. David requested an additional protection order from family court for his safety. The judge declined that request, stating, "You already have a restraining order in place, and it's active for two years. There is no need for another."

After briefly reviewing the recent events, the judge decided they would reconvene in two weeks to determine whether a change of custody was necessary. Brigitte and her attorney immediately began issuing subpoenas to everyone who could testify on her behalf. Gabriel's therapist was included, along with all his previous daycare directors, the current director Gail from his school, and Mrs. Mary, the in-home daycare provider.

Once the hearing began, each witness testified. The judge thanked everyone and announced that she would deliver her ruling the following Monday. For eight long days, Brigitte was on pins and needles, uncertain of what the outcome would be.

A few days later, Brigitte's attorney called and asked her to come down to her office so she could discuss something with her. Brigitte had no idea what her attorney wanted to talk about, but she went anyway to find out. It was then that Brigitte was hit with the most difficult and harsh reality she had ever faced.

Her attorney suggested that Brigitte allow Gabriel to stay with David permanently. She explained it this way: "You now have a criminal record for assault. Let's say your son comes over for the weekend, and while riding his bike he accidentally falls and scrapes his knee. David could use that against you, claiming you're abusing your son—look at his knees, or point to any other injury he might get from normal childhood play. This would open up a whole new issue with the state, and it would not be good for you—not to mention the amount of money you would have to keep spending to defend yourself."

This was something Brigitte certainly didn't need in her life. As sick and sadistic as David was, she knew he would do such a thing out of pure spite, just to hurt Brigitte and destroy her forever. Brigitte was shocked and started to cry. She told her attorney, "I have never been without my son for a long period of time. How will I function without him in my life?"

Her attorney advised her to seek professional counseling, as well as spiritual guidance from her pastor, before making a decision. All the way home, Brigitte cried her eyes out. Yet, as painful as it was, the advice began to make a lot of sense. Since the case had begun, Brigitte and her husband had already spent $30,000 on her attorney and court costs—and that didn't even include the criminal case she was facing. Maybe she thought that if Gabriel did go and live with his dad, perhaps all of this drama could finally settle down and maybe things could get back to normal between her and David.

So Brigitte went to see a family psychiatrist as well as her pastor and first lady of her church. The more Brigitte sat down and explained everything to them, the more everyone seemed to agree that perhaps this was the best solution for everyone. That way, Brigitte could be protected and her husband would not have to endure this nightmare. After all, they had just purchased their first home together, and they needed to get back to being a married couple. This case had tied Brigitte up for so long that she somehow felt that she wasn't always there for Copeland. Although Copeland would miss Gabriel terribly, he understood what her attorney was trying to prevent from happening.

After careful consideration, Brigitte made the toughest decision ever in her life: to let Gabriel go and live with his father. She called her attorney and told her. Her lawyer was surprised and told Brigitte, "You're doing the right thing. Gabriel will be David's full responsibility from now on. And if he let anything happen to Gabriel, he will be in trouble with the state, and you will have your son back again."

Her attorney called David's lawyer and told them that Brigitte was going to let Gabriel live with his dad. Since David was the one typing up all the court appeals and motions, he requested that he wanted Brigitte to have supervised visitations only with their son. This would mean that nobody in Brigitte's family could go and see Gabriel, not even her husband who helped raise him and paid for Gabriel to go to therapy so he could get the help he needed.

Brigitte expected David to be cruel and malicious with this, but she agreed to it to get this case out of the court system once and for all. But in the back of Brigitte's mind, she had already said her goodbyes to her son and prayed to God that he watches over her son and protect him from hurt, harm, or danger since she could no longer be there for him.

Brigitte asked her attorney to do her a huge favor: set up her child support payment through the state, and the attorney general's office could keep track of Brigitte's payments. That way, David wouldn't be able to lie and say he never got them. Brigitte was ordered to pay $300 a month in child support, plus keep her son's health insurance and cover half of his medical bills. She agreed to do all these.

Finally, the case was officially settled and out of the courts, and Brigitte could begin to rebuild her life without Gabriel in it. Since David didn't want any of Brigitte's family to see Gabriel, nor her husband, Brigitte made a conscious choice not to see him as well. She felt it wasn't fair to all the family members who helped her when she first moved back to Texas. David was being evil and cruel as he knew this would hurt her family a lot.

The first two weeks were the most difficult. Brigitte woke each morning without seeing her son or helping him get ready for school. She became depressed and just couldn't seem to pull herself together. Her husband grew extremely concerned and asked her mother to come live with them for a while to help Brigitte.

Her mother stayed for about three or four weeks. The first thing her mom did was make Brigitte get up every morning and take a shower. She cooked breakfast and made Brigitte eat, since she had stopped eating. Finally, her mother had a heart-to-heart talk with her. She told Brigitte that everything that happens to us is all part of God's plan, and that our heavenly Father never puts more on us than we can bear. She went on to say it was for the best that Gabriel went to live with his father. For one, it would give Brigitte time to rebuild her inner strength, as David had done everything in his power to tear her down. Secondly, she deserved some time for herself and to restore her relationship with her husband, since the case put a lot of pressure on them as a couple. She also needed time to replenish and rebuild their savings, as this entire ordeal had cost them $50,000 during the three years Brigitte battled with David in family court.

Brigitte's mother said to her, "I raised you better than that, and you will not let this man defeat you." Hearing those words made sense, but Brigitte had to believe them for herself.

A month passed, and Brigitte made no effort to see Gabriel. Instead, she focused on getting herself together once again. The silence in the house gave Brigitte some peace, allowing her to think and concentrate on her next project.

When David finally realized that Brigitte was not exercising her visitations or calling to talk to Gabriel, he suddenly thought he had made a horrible choice requesting supervised visits. He now understood that Brigitte never had to show up for those. And with Gabriel no longer living with her, David had no access to Brigitte at all. His plan backfired. The woman he loved so much was back to being single again—except this time she was married and living with her husband. The two of them could be happy, moving forward with life without Gabriel.

David knew he had dropped the ball on the entire situation, but he was too proud to admit he had made a mistake. He would never allow Brigitte to be happy; he wanted her to suffer. Suddenly, strange calls began coming to Brigitte's house. On an average day, she received thirty-five to forty calls. Sometimes the callers left messages on her answering machine; other times they hung up. Brigitte contacted their phone company at the time, Southwestern Bell, and had their home number changed. Yet within fifteen minutes the calls would start again.

Brigitte remembered this was the same thing that had happened to her in Tampa when she first moved out of David's home and into her apartment. Late at night, strange knocks came at their front door. The doorbell would ring, and by the time Brigitte looked outside the window, cars were pulling out of the driveway in the early hours after Copeland left for work, leaving her alone. This scared Brigitte, and then it dawned on her—this was David getting back at her for not visiting Gabriel. The harassment and stalking had started all over again.

Now that he was the sole parent, there was no reason for David to call Brigitte. He knew he screwed up big time, but instead of going back to the courts to try and reassess the visits, he didn't want to admit he was wrong or to be made out like a fool.

Over the next several months, David sent countless medical expenses to Brigitte's home for Gabriel. It seemed that once she paid one bill, he would send three or four more. Brigitte realized he was running a scam, taking their son to endless doctor's appointments for everything under the sun. He hoped Brigitte wouldn't pay so he could drag her back into court—using it as an excuse to see her while claiming she's not paying her share of the bills. He didn't care that Gabriel wasn't seeing his mother.

Brigitte had never made David pay to see his child, and she wasn't about to start now. David's heart was hardened. He was desperate to see Brigitte, and over time his obsession grew worse. Brigitte told her mother, "David was blocked and denied access to me for setting up those supervised visits. Now he's livid."

Her mother replied, "He made his bed. Let him lie in it."

Chapter 11

Brigitte Finds Her Peace

As weeks turned into months and months into a year, Brigitte seemed to be going through the motions of everyday life. She often felt alone and empty, missing her son terribly. It had been thirteen months since she last saw him, and David never allowed Gabriel to call the house to speak with her. The silence was devastating. Even though she wasn't seeing her son, she remained under a court order to pay child support to the state.

One day at work, a friend named Barbara—who knew what had happened with Gabriel going to live with David—reached out. Brigitte relied heavily on her family and friends for moral support during that time. Barbara invited Brigitte and Copeland to attend her church for Family and Friends Day. At that time, Brigitte had not been to church in a year; the custody battle had consumed her, leaving little room to seek God's peace.

That Sunday morning, Brigitte and her husband went to church. When the time came to stand and introduce themselves, Brigitte rose and said she and Copeland had been invited by her friend and coworker Barbara. At that moment, Brigitte broke down, crying out before the congregation about what she had endured and how heavily God weighed on her heart. She longed to return to Christ but didn't know where to begin. Brigitte believed Barbara had been sent by

God to invite her back, so she could build a personal relationship with Christ and find a church family.

At the end of the service, Brigitte and her husband joined New Beginning Missionary Baptist Church under the stewardship of Pastor Hyder and his wife, Sister Hyder, the church's first lady. The following Sunday, Brigitte was baptized and reborn as a new creature, a child of God. From the moment, she began her spiritual walk with Christ and became deeply active in the church.

This was the missing piece of Brigitte's life. As a child, she had known of God but never had a personal relationship with him. Brigitte began to read and study the Word and attend Wednesday night Bible study. On some Sundays, she taught Sunday school and became involved in many ministries. She sang in the choir, joined the women's ministry, and, since she loved cooking at home, naturally joined the culinary ministry at the church as well.

It seemed like the more she desired to be at church, the more her life seem to have balance to it. With each passing day without seeing her son, the pain grew a little easier to bear. Brigitte was beginning to regain her strength.

As the Book of Philippians, chapter 4, verse 13, says, "I can do all things through Christ which strengtheneth me," Brigitte's life now had purpose. And she knew she could continue to live. She and her husband were active members of their church, living as a godly married couple should.

Shortly after, however, the evil and wickedness of strange events seemed to continue haunting her, constantly surrounding her. The annoying calls and hang-ups on the phone, the late-night knocks at their front door, and cars pulling up into the driveway, ringing the doorbell, and driving off—all of it began happening again.

Although Brigitte hadn't seen David in over a year, she never imagined she would be stalked beyond her horizons.